14/April/2020

THANK YOU

Dear Friend!

UNTOUCHED BY
HUMAN HANDS IN
PACKAGING!

All Best,

David

INAPPROPRIATE ANAGRAMS

WILD CAVE REDUNDANCY

Inappropriate Anagrams

The Secret Alter Egos of 40 Luminary People in Anagrammatic Poems & Portraits

with Collage Portraits by the Author

DAVID LAWRENCE CUNDY / WILD CAVE REDUNDANCY

HYMNSELF / GUILFORD / 2018

First published in 2018 by
HYMNSELF PUBLISHING
27 Boston Street, Guilford, Connecticut 06437
davidcundyauthor.com

Copyright © 2018 by David Cundy

All rights reserved. No part of this book may be used or reproduced in any manner whatsoever without written permission, except in the case of brief quotations embodied in critical articles and reviews. For information, contact *davidcundyauthor.com/DCA_contact.htm*.

LIBRARY OF CONGRESS CATALOGING-IN-PUBLICATION DATA
Names: Cundy, David, author.
Title: Inappropriate anagrams / by David Cundy.
Description: Guilford, CT. : Hymnself – Publisher, [2018]
Identifiers: LCCN 2018912878| ISBN 9780988680852 (alk. paper) |
ISBN 0988680852 (alk. paper)
LC record available at https://lccn.loc.gov/2018912878

ISBN: 978-0-9886808-5-2

First printing
PRINTED IN THE UNITED STATES OF AMERICA

Inappropriate Anagrams has been designed and illustrated by the author. The fonts are Janson, Modern and Syntax.

Table of Contents (TEN COTTON FABLES)

Introduction	i
HULA MOAN EPÉE – Pele Honua Mea / Madame Pele	2
CAT PAROLE – Cleopatra	4
CHI HEIRS KISS PINS – Princess Shikishi	6
THOU A ZANY CELLO – Nezahualcoyotl	8
SO ANIMAL – Mona Lisa	10
HEN HAS ABS, SIR UMP! – (Missus) Aphra Behn	12
GO! GAG THE ELF – <u>NOW</u>! – Wolfgang Goethe	14
MY EERY HALLS – Mary Shelley	16
AHOY! A THUNDER DIVER – Henry David Thoreau	18
NARWHALS CRIED – Charles Darwin	20
LILTING BUST – Sitting Bull	22
DREAMT HAT – Mad Hatter	24
OH! SATAN'S BUNNY – Susan B. Anthony	26
MS. EEL, UNCLE SAM! – Samuel Clemens / Mark Twain	28
STAY, CAST ARM! – Mary Cassatt	30
ME RADIUM ACE – Madame Curie	32
GURU'S MIND FED – Sigmund Freud	34
BAT RIOT EXPERT – Beatrix Potter	36
TIGER DENTURES – Gertrude Stein	38
HAD ARK FOIL – Frida Kahlo	40
ELITE BANNISTER – Albert Einstein	42
DOLL NAÏF RAN RINKS – Rosalind Franklin	44

YIELD! I LOB HAIL – Billie Holiday	46
NURSE PAM – Superman / George Reeves	48
MORE MARLIN YON! – Marilyn Monroe	50
HER CAROLS CAN! – Rachel Carson	52
DAILY NEWTS: TILDE YAWNS – Walt Disney	54
I INK MR. ANGEL'S TRUTH – (Rev. Dr.) Martin Luther King (Jr.)	56
MUD-CLEAR CHAMP – Marcel Duchamp	58
MARQUEE DAY NOUN – Raymond Queneau	60
MERRY IN HELL – Henry Miller	62
A-BOMB LYRE – Bob Marley	64
SIR OBOES JUGGLER – Jorge Luis Borges	66
AH, LORD YAWN! – Andy Warhol	68
HE'S RODEO LEGIT – Theodor Geisel / Dr. Seuss	70
SIR GEM RESORT – Mister (Fred) Rogers	72
MAGNET RAINS – Agnes Martin	74
MAD HULA IMAM – Muhammad Ali	76
BORN MAZE TRIMMER – Robert Zimmerman / Bob Dylan	78
ANY MAIL? – Maya Lin	80
Acknowledgments	82
Constrained Poetry	84
Citations	86

You are about to enter the delightful linguistic and psychological parallel universe of inappropriate anagrams. Conventional anagrams, which pertinently describe their subjects, are no match for inappropriate ones, which stimulate our subconscious imaginations by surprising us with witty, unexpected connections. Inappropriate anagrams make magic out of words: they transform meaning, constructively rewarding our innate, shared appetite for the novel, and our universal attraction to games of chance. They are endlessly entertaining – humorous, nonsensical, dreamlike, and even a bit psychedelic.

This is a book of anagram-inflected biographical poems, which I call "**SHENANAGRAMS**." The shenanagram is a new form of literary art – one that recognizes a heretofore unappreciated type of anagram and permits its use as legitimate expression, while paying homage to literary and wordplay precedents.

Shenanagrams have rules (see p. 85 for a complete list): Each line incorporates words containing every single letter in the subject's name, and at least one anagram (the second of two consecutive anagrams is set in lightface). Because their text is constrained by these rules, shenanagrams often seem nonsensical (like the poetry of e. e. cummings, Edward Lear or Lewis Carroll, or the prose of Gertrude Stein), so don't worry if you don't always understand them. Shenanagrams may also be enjoyed for their sonic æsthetic, tongue twists and meter.

While inappropriate anagram scenarios are amusing to imagine, seeing them in works of art is transformative: they become (almost) believable! To bring subjects' anagrammatic alter egos to life, I created collage portraits using inappropriate anagrams selected from the poems.

I hope you will enjoy the poetic narratives, anagrammatic zaniness and singular artwork in this premiere collection of Inappropriate Anagrams.

DAVID LAWRENCE CUNDY / WILD CAVE REDUNDANCY
GUILFORD, CONNECTICUT, SEPTEMBER 2018

for Nick *&* Cat

HULA MOAN EPÉE

MADAME PELE (TUTU PELE) (Timeless)   Volcano Goddess
PELE HONUA MEA (Pele of the Sacred Land)
Ka wahine 'ai honua (The Earth-eating Woman)

Volcano worship   in a public place

Tutu Pele, smouldering   **MELD ME A PEA** –
she writes wrath's name   on Kilauea;   **EEL UP**, **TUT**! tuts speedy magma

She danced a **HULA MOAN EPÉE**   she **MADE ME LEAP** (she **MADE ME PALE**)
a *tout le monde* erotic pout   *Was just a dream* – an **EEL-MADE MAP**

She be me shape-shake demoiselle   her hair, her tears, **ME PEALED MA**
a maiden's heaves, a woman's plumes   **DAME EEL AMP** MADE EEL MAP

We touch aforesaid mountain peak   with lava lamps, to **PLEAD A MEME**
Dark clouds' wisps; a heaven's hills   mud-matted scene, **A DAMP MELEE**

INAPPROPRIATE ANAGRAMS

CAT PAROLE

CLEOPATRA (69-30 BC) Queen

Animal magnetism in a public place

Cleopatra, Egypt's queen   **A PEARL COT**

caught Cæsar's plow   **APT ORACLE**, she bore his son

She sailed to Rome in secret, wrapped   **A CARPET, LO**! (It was her ride)

to charm her prey to lover's lane   *Was just a dream – an* **OPAL TRACE**

A temple carving's portraiture   of royalty on **CAT PAROLE**

pale witness to her feline charm   an **ORCA LEAPT**, a **PALACE TOR**

Her story cited with panache   her hieroglyphic **PEARL COAT**

Plethora's dramatic jest?   Her exit, by **A CORAL PET**

INAPPROPRIATE ANAGRAMS

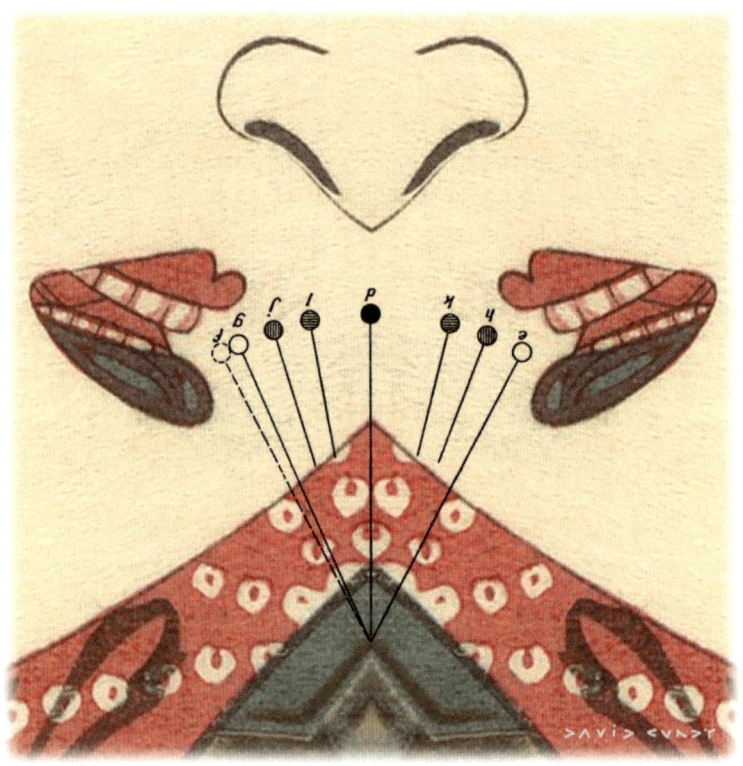

CHI HEIRS KISS PINS

PRINCESS SHIKISHI (1149-1201) Poet / Princess / Nun

The human condition   in a public place

Shikishi *sama*, Princess nun   **HIP SIS SHRINKS ICE**

she – *shijin*, priestess   pinprick shy; **HI! SIS INKS CIPHERS**

Ghostlike fireflies shine, escaping   **SIS, SHE INKS; I CHIRP**, allusive*

This sylphlike *waka*, circumspect   in pillow words: **CHI HEIRS KISS PINS**

With childlike spark sends shivers through us   **PINK CHI IS HERS, SIS**

                                              (SKEINS CHIRP, "HI, SIS!")

Disproving such sensations, thinking   **ICE IS PINK, SIRS. SHH**! (snow fallen)

Praise her achievements, moodlit skies   **[SHH!] I RISK EPIC SINS**, forgetting

hyperconscious, hidden jewels   ink dries, dew beads; **SHIPS SHRINK; ICE IS**

* **SKIP IN, CHERISH SIS**!

INAPPROPRIATE ANAGRAMS

THOU A ZANY CELLO

NEZAHUALCOYOTL (The Hungry Coyote) (1402-1472) Poet / Philosopher / King

Dust to dust in a public place

Poet Nezahualcoyotl   (Day job: king; **LAZE, HOLY TOUCAN!**)
Ephemeral philosophy   (cult analyzed, **LAUNCH OOZY TALE**)

Called *Hungry Coyote*, quetzal plumed   resplendent **COAT, UNHOLY ZEAL**
His poetry called *flowersongs*   chintz calque, a **ZANY TULLE: ACHOO!**

Bedazzlement on counterplay   Shake, **ZANY HULA OCELOT!**
Euphonic oxytocin waltz   play **THOU A ZANY CELLO**: *Bow!*

Lush locutory tongue, amaze   **ALLAY TOUCH ZONE; HAUL ZEN CLAY, TOO!**
Jade flashbulb, syncopated beat   cadenza to **COUNT LOYAL HAZE**

Gloat, hypnotizing cyclotron   eunoia's **LAZY LOAN: TOUCHÉ!**
Zag's ultra-chic technology   zigs, too: **LO, COZY NATAL HUE!**

Laugh, mythologic denizen   in Mesoland (**YEAH, ZONAL CLOUT**)
Glyphs' mezzotint cryptology   applauds: **OHO! ZEN, ACTUALLY!**

INAPPROPRIATE ANAGRAMS

SO ANIMAL

MONA LISA (Lisa Gherardini) (1479-1542)   Portrait Subject
by Leonardo daVinci (1452-1519)

A famous face in a public place

Mona Lisa, portraiture   **A MAN'S OIL**, svelte, **SO ANIMAL**

top A-list paramount celeb   she **NO'S A MAIL**; she **OILS A MAN**

True romance *in italics*, she   a ewe's synapse, **A LAM'S ION**

eyes' starlit egomania   idealized, **MS. I, A-LOAN**

da Vinci, quondam realist   (her smile deceives; yup, **MA'S A LION**)

Scamp Duchamp's lilting acronym   R.S.V.P.? "**NO SAIL, MA**"

Lass timeless, signal, womanly   magnetic, tempting **AS, LO, MAIN**

lasting monarch of the Louvre   **LO, SIN-A-MA**, Madonna G.!

INAPPROPRIATE ANAGRAMS

HEN HAS ABS, SIR UMP!

(MISSUS) **APHRA BEHN** (1640-1689) Playwright / Author / Poet

Pleasure and poetry in a public place

Aphra Behn, dramatist   **HIP SHAMAN'S REBUS** HUMS BRAIN SHAPES
Her mantra – *Carpe noctem* – throbs   its saucy **HAREM'S HIPS-A-BUNS**

Spy, plummy playwright, novelist   (brash **SUSHI MA EARNS PH.B.**!)
"Astrea" – Muses' thighbones' pet   **SHE BUMS PIRANHAS** (jealousy...)

The Rover, play about love's sport   hijinks amuse, **AMBUSH NEARS HIPS**
(Hellena's)...Willmore's troth unpledged   but, tables turned,
                                HARE'S AMBUSH PINS

Prince Oroonoko, banished, luxe   shame's **SHIP BEARS HUMANS** overseas
Crushed royal slave his nymph beheads(!)   **HARSH NIMBUS PEAS**
                                (**SHH! SUNBEAMS PAIR**!)

"The Disappointment" (smart blue rhyme)   So? **HE'S A SHRIMP; A SNUB**
                                (downtime...)
Her woman's point of view abashed   lust stops: no **SPARS IN BUSH** (**AHEM!**)

Hosannahs! Wolf upbore her fame   (This **HEN HAS ABS, SIR UMP**! She *does!*)
launched women's birthright to speak minds   (to **HUSH A PRISM'S BEAN** a crime)

Westminster Abbey resting place   chic, humorous (**BRAIN'S ASHES HUMP!**)
Wit's flesh, bound (mortality)   rephrased: **ABS PERISH, HUMANS!** (*sigh*)

INAPPROPRIATE ANAGRAMS

GO! GAG THE ELF – <u>NOW</u>!

WOLFGANG GOETHE (1749-1832) Polymath

The sale of one's soul in a public place

Wolfgang Goethe, polymath   **EGGNOG OF WEALTH**
arranging flowers   the Oh-Gee, **THE NEW GO-GO FLAG**

Groundshaking life's work, staggering   as **HE OF TOGGLE GNAW** foresaw
for the young Werther, long ago   romance with death (**HOW LONG, FATE EGG?**)

Faust's downfall – no outbargaining   his houseguest (**GONG THE EGO FLAW!**)
Apprentice, hangdog afterwards   "technologist" (**FOOL! GNAW THE EGG!**)

With color's language, forge ahead   **NTH AGE OF OWL EGG** has dawned
Theatergoers follow, nagged   **GO! GAG THE ELF – NOW**! *Zugzwang* rules!

INAPPROPRIATE ANAGRAMS

MY EERY HALLS

MARY SHELLEY (1797-1851) Author

How technology will save us   in a public place

Mary Shelley, I am she   **AY, HELL, YES, MR.**, ALLEYS RHYME

I wrote my name on mem'ry's hill   a **LYE SHY REALM**, MY LEERY LASH

Grey modern day Prometheus   pallbearing **ALL MY HERESY**

my idyll's moral chemistry   a daymare in **MY EERY HALLS**

Ye marshallers of industry   **HELL'S ARMY, YE**, Y'ALL HEM RYES

machin'ry heartlessly blasphemes   **RALLY, YE HEMS**! MY LYRE HEALS!

Romanticism heavenly   yields **MAY RYE SHELL** and **YEARLY HELMS**

I, telepath, lay cryptograms   **AM SLYLY HERE**: SERF TAKEN INN

INAPPROPRIATE ANAGRAMS

AHOY! A THUNDER DIVER

HENRY DAVID THOREAU (1817-1862) Philosopher / Author

A different drummer in a public place

Henry David Thoreau, thinker   **AHOY! A THUNDER DIVER** deep
apocryphal staunch daredevil   (*a* **HEADY, DRIVEN AUTHOR,** *Chief*)

Charmed, vaunted pencil factory heir   he **HUNTED AVIARY HORDE**
fey rebel 'gainst drained hours' thieves   (*Mark's* **TV HOUR HANDY, DEARIE!**)

Rad, trenchant psychosurgeon thrived   in **RENOVATED DAIRY (HUH?)**
that everything be simply done   crusade **DROVE AIRY HEADHUNT** (*Kewl!*)

At *Walden*, drivethrough countermyth   (*Do* **HOVER, HAUNTED DIARY!**)
rare, divagated thoughts; two years   lived in **A HARDENED IVORY HUT**

Harped *quiet desperation lives*   (Why?) (**DAD, TRY HOURI HEAVEN** – *Bliss!*)
synoptic thread, harsh verdict stunned   (**OH, ARTY DRUID HEAVEN** – *Not!*)

Trounced bodhisattva fatherly   **VERANDAH HOUR DEITY**
thought everything had *dear life price*   (**HAVE RUDDY ANTIHERO** *now?*)

Had contretemps: didn't pay tax share   (*Guv* **ONE RUDE, IVY HARDHAT**, *blunt*)
did protest slavery and war   Hush! (**UH, OH: DREARY DEVIANT?**)

Viceroy of education rich   *heard music:* **HEAVY RONDEAU (THIRD...)**
Dude's transcendental, traveling voice   his hymns **HIVED AURA THRENODY**

In time's stream fished; truths live today   (**AT HEAVY RHINO UDDER?** *Nah.*)
preached *don't kill time*, "Forever Yours"   (*Whoa!* **VERY HAUNTED HAIRDO**, *Hank!*)

INAPPROPRIATE ANAGRAMS

NARWHALS CRIED

CHARLES DARWIN (1809-1882)   Scientist

Hiding in plain sight... in a public place

Charles Darwin, he's on board   **SHREWD CRANIAL**, he sailed to
Galapagos, charmed isle renowned   with **NAIL HARD CREWS**, ARCH WISER LAND

The sacred shaken in the world   **HIS CRAWLER DNA** foretold
where magic hands bear fool's gold   *Was just a dream* – **A DANCER'S WHIRL**

The priest class draws the line and throws   bell, book at him, **A CANDLE WHIRRS**
as charily he downed the scheme   a pyramid, a **LAW CARD SHRINE**

We reach said origins atilt   **A CHILDREN'S WAR** that rages on
Watching from said Tree of Life   upon his death, the **NARWHALS CRIED**

INAPPROPRIATE ANAGRAMS

LILTING BUST

SITTING BULL (1831-1890) Chief

West meets West in a public place

Sitting Bull, Lakota Sioux   Do **GLINT, LIT SUB**, brave **LILTING BUST**
with grittiness applaudable   of thee I sing, and **LIT BINS' GLUT**!

Intransigent, unflappable   with Winchester (*Don't* **BUTT IN, GILLS**!)
at Little Bighorn beat U.S.   a shutout score, so **TING IT, BULLS**!

Disintegration doubtlessly   a fait accompli; **SIGN BILL, TUT**!
withstanding tribulations cold   chew frozen food, as **BUGS TILL TIN**!

Out Wild Westing, eagle bold   majestic chieftain; **BILL TUGS TIN**!
transmitting goodwill beautifully   gave autographs, so **SLIT GILT BUN**!

At Standing Rock from bullets died   arrest attempt; use **BIN SLUG; TILT**!
ghost dancing trouble took his life   a **BLUING STILT**, when **LUNG BIT SILT**

Substantial if intangible   his culture vanished; **STUN, GLIB LIT**
Natives libelled; "history" judged   No consolation (**GIST: I'LL BUNT**)

INAPPROPRIATE ANAGRAMS

DREAMT HAT

[The] **MAD HATTER** (1865-) Fictional Character
from Alice's Adventures in Wonderland by Lewis Carroll (1832-1898)

Rhyme and unreason in a public place

Liddell's Hatter, barking mad   **HATTED RAM** in Wonderland
made nonsense rhymes from little bats,   from writing desks, from spun **TAM THREAD**

Confrères had tea at six pm   **HAD MATTER** vital to discuss
rotated settings whimsically   *Was just a dream – that dream*, **DREAMT HAT**

He rambled mathematically   (undoubtedly was **RED AT MATH**)
The March Hare and the Dormouse vexed   (still, Alice couldn't get **RAD AT THEM**)

In this style, daft, mercurial   (poor Alice knew she'd **MET RAD HAT**)
Adventures in semantics when   she saw the man in **THE RAD TAM**

INAPPROPRIATE ANAGRAMS

OH! SATAN'S BUNNY

SUSAN B. ANTHONY (1820-1906) Abolitionist / Women's Rights Activist

Gender equality in a public place

Susan B. (Ms.) Anthony   **OH! SATAN'S BUNNY** HAUNTS YON BANS

Bold hootenanny suffragettes   **NAY AT SNUBS, HON**, Sentinels

Unmasks outlandish binary   **ANNOY, STUN, BASH** her strategy

no labyrinth unpassable   **HAST ANY NOUNS, B.**? JUSTICE, RIGHTS!

Her supernova buoyantness   **B. ASHY ANT ON SUN**? *No way*

annoyed by halftone dinosaurs   **NTH SNOB? NAY, U-S-A**! Okay!

No "thank you" banners standing by   'twas only fair, **AUNT BONNY SASH**

Thorny banes shun ERA   **NTH USA BANS YON**; Fight On!

INAPPROPRIATE ANAGRAMS

MS. EEL, UNCLE SAM!

SAMUEL CLEMENS (MARK TWAIN) (1835-1910) Author

The Laughter Cure   in a public place

Samuel Clemens, humorist   **MR. AT-A-WINK**, known prankster

Malarkey-watching skeptic's plume   **CALM MULES SEEN**; SMALL EMU SCENE!

Wheelman plumbs shallows (nice pen name)   Crew's **MEN SMELL SAUCE**;
                                                           MEN CUSS ELM ALE!

"Mark twain" sculpts earmarked waterline   **SEAS CULL ME, MEN**! Seize **MINK-AT-WAR**!

Tom's paintwork hustle, hallmark scheme   spelunking secrets, **WARM AT INK**

Aunt Polly helmless, gimcracks waived   escaped again, **MS. SCALENE MULE**!

Huck's landmark melee showboat trip   (**CLUELESS MEN, MA**! ALL-MEME CENSUS)

embarked with tailwinds, luck's friend Jim   slave seeking freedom, **KARMA TWIN**

Sir Kay with Yank in Camelot   Eclipse numbs **MS. EEL, UNCLE SAM**!

time traveller's framework manuscript   **RANK WIT, MA**: science fiction tale

At mausoleum, luminesce   your swank **ENAMEL MUSCLES** flex

Territory lies ahead   amusements call; *Wake*, **ARK WIT MAN**!

INAPPROPRIATE ANAGRAMS

STAY, CAST ARM!

MARY CASSATT (1844-1926) Artist

Maternal attachment in a public place

SRTA. M, YA CATS!	Mary Cassatt, impressionist	**MA'S ARTSY CAT**
MS. A, CAT SATYR	Art's armchair myth	compassionate, (**MY STARS! A CAT**!)
MS. R: CATS AT YA!	Rouge daydream æsthetician, she	(**MY CARATS SAT** on **TARMAC STAYS**)
MS. Y: A CAT'S ART	Yin's talents asymmetrical	(to **ACT SMART, SAY,** AS MY ARTS ACT)
MS. C, ARTY AS A T	Crayon staccatos, smudged pastels	**MS. C'S ART AT YA!** (STAY, CAST ARM!)
SCARY TAT, MS. A!	As luminary catalyst Edgar Degas	(**MY, CAST A STAR**!)
A RACY TAT, MS. S!	Snobs, mannerly aristocrats	strewed patronage, **CATTY AS MARS**
AY, MS. S, CAT ART	Slung marvy cotton parachutes	(So down to earth!) See, **STARS MAY ACT**!
MS. A, STRAY CAT	A stagecraft's distaff imagery – "The Child's Bath"	(**MY CAT'S A TSAR**!)
MS. T, CAT'S-A-RAY	trends warmly, systematically	(Through abstract rhymes, **CATS' ARMY SAT**)
CAST A RAY, MS. T!	Twee primate satisfaction yields ennoblement;	**TA-TA, MY SCARS**!

INAPPROPRIATE ANAGRAMS

ME RADIUM ACE

MADAME CURIE (Maria Salomea Sklodowska) (1867-1934) Scientist

The discovery of polonium in a public place

Madame Curie, scientist   **ME RADIUM ACE**

a medium   her name acclaimed: **DAME ICE-A-RUM**

Made research in elysium   a **MUM DICE AREA**, fraught with risk

Her mettle and achievements proud   (**DARE I, MUM ACE**, lift lyre to thee?)

The XYs fumed dramatically   opposed her with **A MERMAID CUE**

True academic amazon   she would prevail, **A DUE MIME ARC**

Her diaries much too warm to touch   **MUD AREA MICE** (UM, MARE-A-DICE?)

Get well soon, dream cranium   **ME AURA MEDIC**: CURE DAME AIM!

INAPPROPRIATE ANAGRAMS

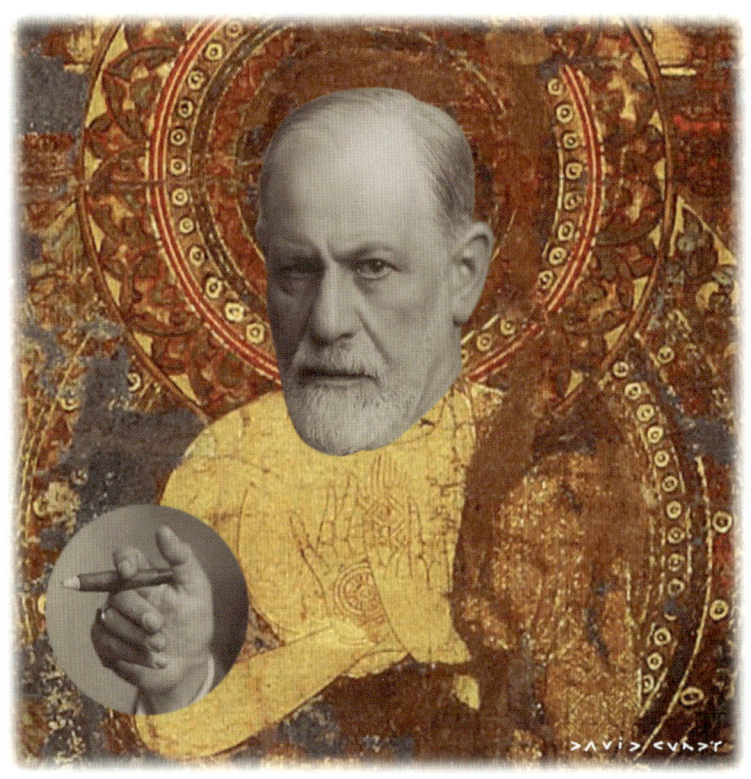

GURU'S MIND FED

SIGMUND FREUD (1856-1939) Psychoanalyst

The analysis of the mind in a public place

Sigmund Freud, the headshrinker   **DUG DENIM SURF**
DUG FEMUR DINS   UNDID FUR GEMS, **DUG DERMIS FUN**

He dreamed of disguised urgencies   of **UDDERS FUMING,** MUD GUNS FIRED
as mundane wildfires wigs consumed   (*A sleepwalk, that – a* **FUSED MIND RUG**)

The super-ego's mute, in fact   offended by the **ID-FUMED RUNGS**
grim ladder of subconsciousness   the **GURU'S MIND FED,** DIM FUDGE RUNS

Grew mindful, worried for our fates   defaulting to **ME** / **FUN** / **DRUGS** / **ID**
Frisson gummed up by discontent   Predicted future? **US, FIRMED DUNG**

INAPPROPRIATE ANAGRAMS

BAT RIOT EXPERT

BEATRIX POTTER (1866-1943) Author / Illustrator / Scientist

R_xterminating pests   in a public place

Beatrix Potter – storybooks   **BAT RIOT EXPERT**, naturally
furred tetrapod exhibitor   (If **OTTER PIX BE ART**, so smart!)

Tot Peter Rabbit's droll faux pas   **PET BRAT – OR EXIT**! (a tight squeeze)
brash carrot-topped exorbitance   (Lettuce: **R_x TO BAIT PETER**)

Imp Nutkin's leaf troop bateaux purred   Acorns? **BAIT – OR PRETEXT**, riddled
exuberating pirouettes   (If rodents, **TREETOP BAIT R_x**)

Keen, ambidextrous portraiture   connecting **TEAPOT TRIBE R_x**
mouse, rabbit, duck, newt, tortoise pix   (Odd: no known **TAROT BERET PIX**!)

Reputed artist, textbook's foil   **A BETTER OX TRIP** *à là carte*
Posterity, be proximate!   (*Bad mice?* **TRITE BOA PET R_x**!)

INAPPROPRIATE ANAGRAMS

TIGER DENTURES

GERTRUDE STEIN (1874-1946) Author

Free association   in a public place

Gertrude Stein? Word: She arose   Of literati, she **REIGNED TRUEST**
entrusted, wearing **TIGER DENTURES**   smart suede ingrate, **RUDE, RESETTING**

language, she the *maîtresse* driest   **ETUDE STRINGER,** RINGED TRUSTEE
reframed the general glue and gist   *Was just a dream – a* **GREEN DUST RITE**

Skeene's button, Georgine's radical   **ITS TENDER URGE,** ITS NUDE REGRET
Miss Helen Furr's tinged merkin patch   **SIR TENTED URGE,** SIR RUG DÉTENTE

peruse said gentle masterpiece   its voice in fine **TUNED REGISTER**
Glitter, glazed by zen duress   a **GUTTERED SIREN** ENDS TRITE URGE

INAPPROPRIATE ANAGRAMS

HAD ARK FOIL

FRIDA KAHLO (1907-1954) Artist

Self-portrait of the soul   in a public place

Frida Kahlo: Oeuvre surreal   Her **DAHLIA FORK**
played ace of hearts   like **ID LOAF: HARK**! HARK! OIL FAD!

Charmed by her brave if reckless cool   El Hombre said, **AH, FLORA, KID**!
She daily took on fresh allure   *her every dream* **A FAKIR HOLD**

On azure skies she painted life   enduring pain, **HAD FRAIL OK**
shared starkest minings of her soul   (**IF HALO DARK**, she **HAD ARK FOIL**)

Of pride in her vicarious   let's speak of days when **FOLK HAD AIR**
Masterstrokes from her mind's eyes   laid junglesful **OF HAIL, DARK**

INAPPROPRIATE ANAGRAMS

ELITE BANNISTER

ALBERT EINSTEIN (1879-1955) Physicist

The practice of physics   in a public place

Albert Einstein, EmCee Squared   a mensch, an **ELITE BANNISTER**
true able trust in G*d, not dice   a seer, **A BENT RESILIENT**

Then relative, his subtle means   took **TRANSIT BEELINE** to his end
warping space / blueprinting time   *his dreamt-of* **NETTLE BINARIES**

The base electron was his friend   his **TINIEST ENABLER**
his noblest nature periods dot   **NINE TABLE RITES,** NINE BITS RELATE

We celebrate instinctively   his quantum leap, **NINE BEERS ATILT**
Black rain, in counterpoint, inheres   discharging **LINEN BATTERIES**

INAPPROPRIATE ANAGRAMS

DOLL NAÏF RAN RINKS

ROSALIND FRANKLIN (1920-1958) Scientist

Decoding DNA in a public place

Rosalind Franklin, chemistress   by Ouija, **FINLAND'S IRON LARK**
dark lioness of Gene & Tea   God's girlfriend (ex) (**DRINKS RAINFALL, NO?**)

Branch: X-ray crystallography   Key finding: **DOLL NAÏF RAN RINKS**
in Bildungsroman's lakefront lab   **I SNARL FOR DNA LINK** (GRRR!)

Discovery's philanthropoid   Full nickname: **NIL-NIL FORKS-A-DARN**
Took ironclad *Photo Fifty-one*   learned structure's hints (**RINKS NOD: RAINFALL!**)

"Lent" Crick and Watson fieldwork   "Why You Are You" – **FINN, KRILL AND OARS**
(Bond, craftsmanlike angelic pair   **FALL IN! DRINK SONAR!** *Do*, old chaps!)

CAT G bound helix uncials   farmworking, **DRANK IN FLORAL SIN**
Lacks' doornail cells, and dragonflies   and gremlin's **SNAIL DRANK FLORIN** (*how?*)

Fair Dolly asks (e'er winning *baa*)   "Sa-ay, wha-at if **FIRS DRANK LANOLIN?**"
Purloined blanketflowers align   so *Cheers!* **DRAIN LION FLASK, RN**!

INAPPROPRIATE ANAGRAMS

YIELD! I **LOB** HAIL

BILLIE HOLIDAY (1915-1959) Singer

Who's got her own in a public place?

Billie Holiday, chanteuse   a **HOLY IDLE ALIBI**

You are *the child* implausible   **YE, A LIBIDO HILL** of song

Sweet little things, you boldly wailed   now **I DEAL HILLY BIO** dim

Sighed *Love will make you do things* brash   **LYE OIL BID HAIL**! YIELD! I <u>LOB</u> HAIL

Your smile just beams, childlike   **HI! I BADE LILY, LO** (*Hello?*)

A little moonbeam: devilishly   **I HOLD LYE ALIBI** near vest

Say *I'll get by,* Miss Lady Day   with choir **I AD LIB HOLY LIE**

Travellin' light (*he said goodbye*)   **BY HALO LID I LEI**; *Fi-ne*

INAPPROPRIATE ANAGRAMS

NURSE PAM

SUPERMAN (1938-) Comic Book Hero
George Reeves (1914-1959) Actor

Superhero, incognito in a public place

George Reeves, actor, Superman   **SUN, MR. APE**

star televised, permutable   exaggeration: **MAN, PER US**

Left Krypton, Smallville's wunderkind   geologer (the **MAN'S PURE**, sure!)

used doppelgänger secretive   (Clark Kent more classy than **SAM PRUNE**)

Glum shirtsleeve steganographer   the *Daily Planet's* **SANER UMP**

at loggerheads with thieveries   Mack spring/sprang/sprung, donned **RAN-ME-UPS**

~~A bird! A plane!~~ A flying fish   smug diving pose: **SEA – MR. PUN**!

Protect us from mass impotence   (Cue up Atomic Age, **NURSE PAM**!)

Expressive wondermonger guy   (scan **MENU, SPAR**; go, **RAP 'EM, SUN**!)

saved Lois Lane, maid waterlogged   found x-ray specs in his **MAN PURSE**

Egregious crimes vexed Man of Steel   flipped Mxy's **RUNE MAPS**, backwardly

Theatergoing servicemen   hope (wishful) he will **REMAP SUN**

INAPPROPRIATE ANAGRAMS

MORE MARLIN YON!

MARILYN MONROE (1945-1962) Actress

The symbolism of sex in a public place

Actress Marilyn Monroe   **ROAR, NYLON MIME!** MORE MARLIN YON!
incomparably enormous star   (wrong cookie: "**MANY MINOR ROLE**")

By charming pheromone appeal   (not **ONLY MR. ROMAINE**, dear)
Triumphant posy moonflower   bared **MIRY NEON MOLAR**, more

Blonde bombshell's legendary limbs   curved gams **IN MELON ARMORY**
erotomanic salarymen   her pin-up splayed (**MOAN, MERRY LOIN!**)

Admirers, many; lovers, known   (Fine, **MARRY MOON LINE**, if you must)
made movies lyrical, renowned   *Some Like It Hot* – **MY LEMON [OR] RAIN**

Miss Norma Jeane, misunderstood   (Fly, bluebirds; **MANNERLY I ROOM**)
Foredooming early omens missed   checked out of **ORAL MEMORY INN**

INAPPROPRIATE ANAGRAMS

HER CAROLS CAN!

RACHEL CARSON (1907-1964)   Environmentalist / Journalist / Author

Environmental protection agency in a public place

Rachel Carson saved your life   with **ANCHORS CLEAR**
'stute journalist *chère raconteuse*, a **SCHOLAR CRANE**

Original, core activist   she **RAN CARE LOCHS**, RANCH ORACLES
Observer with élan, cachet   **HER CORAL CANS** ARC NOËL'S ARCH

Environmental outreach acts   a *Silent Spring*, **A CORNER CLASH**
used science, researched chemicals   found poisoners – **ERR, CHAOS CLAN**

All nature's forceful attachée   **SHE, COLA CAR RN** for Earth
Humanist, declared to care   as **ARCH CO'S LEARN**, HER CAROLS CAN!

INAPPROPRIATE ANAGRAMS

DAILY NEWTS: TILDE YAWNS

WALT DISNEY (1901-1966)   Animator

Freezing frames in a public place

Disney, Walt: Iconic eye   draws **DAILY NEWTS**

cels watchable   with Huey, Lou' and **SAINTLY DEW**'

From Mickey, waltzing destiny   **AW, TIDY LENS**! SEW, TINY LAD!

wealth density in Minnie-ature   (**YES, WILD ANT,** I WED SLY ANT)

Dwarves doing cartwheels splendidly   '**TIS LADY, NEW**! WIT LADS' YEN! (Whew!)

were syndicated planetwide   (on Pluto, too – a **DAINTY SLEW**)

Laughworthy serendipity   with wagtail Goofy (**SIT**; **LYE DAWN**!)

Speak, *Fantasia's* tiddlywinks!   As Goethe groans, a **TILDE YAWNS**

INAPPROPRIATE ANAGRAMS

I INK MR. ANGEL'S TRUTH

[Rev. Dr.] **MARTIN LUTHER KING** [Jr.] (1929-1968)   Civil Rights Activist / Minister

Prayer for a dream   in a public place

Reverend Doctor M.L. King   Hark! **I INK MR. ANGEL'S TRUTH**
Kind man, great faith; now let us pray   **KNIGHT MARLIN TRUE**, to honor you

In Birmingham white cruelty   shocked U.S.A.: **ARM LINK TRUE THING**
in march through *water*, looking up   Jim Crow went down: **MILE-RANKING TRUTH**

In D.C., August, 'Sixty-three   Black dreaming (**REM INK TRUTH, ALIGN!**)
Equality and brotherhood   God's kingdom come: **LINE-MARKING TRUTH**

Almighty Christian, anti-war   took peaceful path: **KILN-REAMING TRUTH**
Nobelist, history-making Heart   speak to us, **MINK ALIGNER, TRUTH**!

Your birth thy nation's holiday   remaking us: **MAN, RING LIKE TRUTH**!
Peal, Chimes of Freedom, ringing out   keep brothers, **RIG-LINK TRUTH! AMEN**

INAPPROPRIATE ANAGRAMS

MUD-CLEAR CHAMP

MARCEL DUCHAMP (1887-1968) Artist

The modernization of art in a public place

Marcel Duchamp, bona fide   you **MUD-CLEAR CHAMP**
nailed porcelain   trimmed cuttlefish for **CARP-MADE MULCH**

Herd camel campus retinal: you vaporized its **CREAM CLAD HUMP**
Femme bride descends, the fountain claps   R. Mutt so signs, a **CLAMP-CURED HAM**

Miss Mona, *personne chaude au cul*   maid ready with **HER MAD CLAM CUP**
Rose Sélavy, dry camp *charmeuse*   punned "Love is life," beat **CALM PEACH DRUM**

Come, champion perdurable   **ME MADCAP CHURL**, ME ARCH PLUM CAD
Thy last act cryptic, mummified   *Étant donnés* – Peep, **LAMP-CUED CHARM**!

INAPPROPRIATE ANAGRAMS

MARQUEE DAY NOUN

RAYMOND QUENEAU (1903-1976) Author / Poet

A game of words   in a public place
(**Un jeu de mots**   *dans une place publique*)

Raymond Queneau, psychopomp   **MARQUEE DAY NOUN**
you made your name   "in quotes," **YE AQUA NEON DRUM**

Odd language arts your mental quest   arranged in **ANY RANDOM QUEUE**
constrained by quirts and question marks   a QWERTY dream –
                              MUNDANE QUAY ROE

Thus qualms in prose and poetry   sit at her feet, **AROUND QUEEN MAY**
quaff beauty and modernity   **NUDE MORAY QUEAN**: MARAUD YON QUEEN!

Quick fox reshuffling x-array   *Cent mille milliards* **QUEUE NOMAD YARN**
taut lipograms and palindromes   required by **A QUERN NAMED YOU**

INAPPROPRIATE ANAGRAMS

MERRY IN HELL

HENRY MILLER (1891-1980) Author

The plucking of zithers in a public place

Henry Miller, belletrist **MERRY IN HELL**

or anywhere in limelight, **MR. HELL-IN-RYE**

In everything, embellisher *outré;* **HE, MR. LYRE NIL**

mesmerically extravagant hypnotic tales – **NIL EEL MYRRH**

Gave honey Tania, mellivore arpeggios to **LIMN HER LYRE**

Keypuncher masculine (read: male) **RE: HYMEN RILL**... HILLY MEN ERR

Wry, trenchant, superluminal hymnographer, **EL RHYMER NIL**

Court stenography laments: Look! There is no **ELL IN RHYMER**

INAPPROPRIATE ANAGRAMS

A-BOMB LYRE

BOB MARLEY (1945-1981) Singer / Songwriter / Musician

Another song of freedom in a public place

Hail up, Bob Marley, Rasta man   **MY ABLE BRO**, MY BAR-BE-LO

Mount Zion's barb empyreal   **BY AMBER, LO**, ALB EMBRYO

The *movement*, bibliography   sing **BLOB-RAY-ME** with I 'n' I

Wail *woe yoe yoe*, blacks reggae lamb   Jah's *jammin' soldier*, **LOBBY MARE**

You *stand up*, stubborn, comradely   **YO, MR. BABEL** – *Babylon!*

Redemption doubt, brave clergyman   a sharp, *small axe*, an **A-BOMB LYRE**

Affirmatively ribboning   the **BALMY ROBE** of righteousness

'xemplary, broadminded bard   salve **BLEARY MOB**! *One heart, one love!*

INAPPROPRIATE ANAGRAMS

SIR OBOES JUGGLER

JORGE LUIS BORGES (1899-1986) Author / Poet

Magical realism on trial in a public place

Dear Señor Borges (Jorge Luis),

On docket: Case, **SIR OBOES JUGGLER**
Orbs v. Joggers; juries called   selecting you **BIG EGOLESS JUROR**

Your **BIG LORE SURE JOGS** our small brains   you *"y sí"* **SOLO REBUS JIGGER**
Your *Book of Sand* – **LO, RUBIES, JOGGERS!**   Their *grande* **EGOS BLUR JOG, SIRE**

BLUE OGRES JOG, SIR (*Sí, Señor*)   **OUR GIRLS' BEES JOG**, *además*
Loco **RUBES RIG JOGS**: ¡OLÉ!   **JURIES, LO, ROB EGGS**: Ixnay!

RUGS LIE, ERGO JOBS. All rise!   **BOORS SURE JIGGLE**: Guilty eyes
JOB SURGERIES LOG evidence   **RUG BEES ROIL JOGS**: Now *that's* intense!

RIG JOGS BLUE ORES: Prime suspect   **SOUL BEERS JOG RIG**: I object!
ROSES RUE GLIB JOG: Sustained   (**OUR SOBER JIGGLES** overruled)

BURGS JEER IGLOOS: Gaveled down   **GIGOLOS JEER RUBS**, the clowns
SORE OBI JUGGLERS testify   **BOLEROS URGE JIGS**: Alibi

JOGS OR BEGUILERS? Plaintiff rests   **JOULES OR BIG ERGS**? Jury's out
SURE, BOIL JOGGERS! Verdict's in

Sincerely Yours,
SIR JOULES EGG ORB

P.S.: **EGGS LIE. JUROR, SOB**

INAPPROPRIATE ANAGRAMS

AH, LORD YAWN!

ANDY WARHOL (1928-1987) Artist

Art, as car crash in a public place

Andy Warhol, Pop Artiste   Say **AH, LORD YAWN**! (OH, WANLY RAD!)
Incendiary wigwam louche   electric chairman (**DARN YA, HOWL**!)

A languid wary lordship, his   Prince Brillo Box, **A WRY LAD, HON**
the art world's playground chancellor   Miss Empire State, **LADY WHO RAN**

No ordinary marshmallow   Saint Silver Clouds (**AH, RANDY OWL**!)
wore shockable androgyny   in pale toupée, the **WAN LORD HAY**

A workaholic dynamo   Duke Capsule Time would **WANLY HOARD**
adept in whirlpool wizardry   "Screen Test" auteur did **HOLD WAN RAY**

Showed Campbell's Soup and Marilyn   **HOLY AND RAW**, the Pope of Camp
with Factory girls and Superstars   their Drella dear (**WAN HALO, DRY**!)

Mythologized and praiseworthy   on earthly plane (**HA**! **ANY WORLD**...)
in wetwear's dainty echelons   his fifteen minutes **HAD LORN WAY**

INAPPROPRIATE ANAGRAMS

HE'S RODEO LEGIT

THEODOR GEISEL (DR. SEUSS) (1904-1991) Author / Illustrator

Fun fish and fairness in a public place

Theo Geisel, Dr. Seuss   top hat, **HE'S RODEO LEGIT**
A sisterhood evangelist   (**OHO! T.G. IS RED EEL**, yes!)

With thoroughbred delightfulness   **SIR GEE LED HOOT**; he **HELD GOOSE RITE**
and otherworldly juggleries –   **THREE IDLE GOOS**, EIGHT EEL DOORS

He, allegories' altruist   promoted **RED ETHOLOGIES**
enlightened humans' brotherhood   (**LOST GEODE HEIR**, IT'S HERE, OLE DOG!)

Kind Horton's tender guilelessness   **GOD'S ELITE HERO** (OOH, SLEET DIRGE!)
Sly **HOT ROD ELEGIES** intrigue   McElligot's: **HE DIGS REEL, TOO**

Though Yertle's ukase meaningless   proclaimed (sure) **I, THE GOD – OR ELSE**
deposed of his regalities   now here's **TO ETHER EGO LID**

Housecleaning creature, chapeau shod   (**SIR TEE HELD GOO**; SIR GEE HELD, TOO)
[**GOO LISTED HERE**: HERE'S TILDE GOO!   **HE LETS GOO RIDE**: 'TIS RED GOO. HEEL!]

The Grinch, rude sour malcontent   **LO! SEE GOTH RIDE** HEIST OGRE LODE
enlightened, saw through doltish ways   **GOTH LED SOIREE**... THE DEER SLEIGH, TOO!

Sam, gourmet chef extraordinaire   would limit choice: **HOG DIET – OR ELSE**
Digestive, he persuaded, too   Why, looky! **O! HERE'S DIET LOG!**

Lorax abode? His single tree   (**OOH, GELID TREES**, DO TIE LOGS HERE!)
proclaimed him seedling optimist   **HIS LOG TREE ODE**, HIS ROOTED GLEE

Seuss, unsurpassed in wondrousness   (Oh, **SUDSERS**, DRESS US in suspenders!)
Just deserts, absurdness themed   **SO DO THE EEL RIG**, dourness!

INAPPROPRIATE ANAGRAMS

SIR GEM RESORT

MISTER ROGERS (Fred Rogers) (1928-2003) Children's TV Educator

A welcoming neighbor on public television

Mister Rogers, minister   of minds, sirs, he, **SIR GEM RESORT**
Affirmative's encourager   'midst **REMS' ROTE RIGS** and **TERRIERS' SMOG**

His taxidermies' merry thoughts   when children guessed, "**ERR... TIGER MOSS?**"
ventriloquism's groovy stripes   "Why, **RIMS OR EGRETS**; STIR MORE ERGS!"

Smart allegories dramatized   "**GET, MISS OR ERR**, EGRESS OR TRIM,"
when Dreamtime's lost geographers   **REGRESS TO RIM** (REGRETS, SIR OM)

To germinate progressive growth   the **MEREST RIGORS** RIG ROSE TERMS
This brightsome, stronger altruist   helped kids smell roses, **TRIM ROSE ERGS**

INAPPROPRIATE ANAGRAMS

MAGNET RAINS

AGNES MARTIN (1917-2004) Artist

The transcendence of time in a public place

Agnes Martin: seer serene **SAINT ENGRAM**, she

she made her name on waiting walls, in **MAGNET RAINS**

She painted with monastic grip an understated **TANGRAM SINE**

a grasp of mere infinity *Was just a dream – where* **MANTAS REIGN**

Art, agnostic and aflame synchronic with its **A-STRING NAME**

forgot its manners axial **NEAT** MINARET, its **MARGINS** SANG

We gaze at aforementioned walls assembled in the **SAME ANT RING**

Wanting base relief, we may escape to her **ENIGMA'S TARN**

MAD HULA IMAM

MUHAMMAD ALI (1942-2016)   Heavyweight Boxing Champion

The promotion of boxing in a public place

Muhammad Ali: Greatest: Champ **A MAD MAUL, HIM**
demolished men **MAD HULA IMAM**, taunts acclaimed

Sure method, most grammatical poetically to **HAM, LAUD, MAIM**
left butterfly, right apian he hammered 'em – **HIM DUAL, MA'AM**!

Charmed, aimful jungle rumble man **HAM À LÀ MUM ID**, thrilla saint
unmatched, immaculate in style **HAIL, MUM ADAM**! LAUD HIM, MAMA!

Untrammeled masher (liar *not*) [**DUH,**] **I, A MAMMAL**? [HA!] I AM MUM, LAD!
Punchlines made a sad Rome smile (**I HUM LAM-A-DAM** For The Win!)

INAPPROPRIATE ANAGRAMS

BORN MAZE TRIMMER

BOB DYLAN (ROBERT ZIMMERMAN) (b. 1941)   Singer / Songwriter / Musician

It's zen minus zero in a public place

Cast of characters

MR. T-Z RAN BEE RIM. OM!	Dylan, Bob: Shy noblest played **MR. TIMBRE ZERO, MAN**
MR. REM: TONEARM BIZ.	verbigeration summarized named **MR. ZOMBIE REM** RANT, he
MR. I-T-Z RAN BEER, MOM.	Cobweb's encyclopedia **MR. IAMB TREMOR ZEN**, Esquire
	famed bamboo pretzel mirror man an alphabet: *Why* **BAN BOLD Y**?
MR. O RAN MEET BIZ, MR.	A native-**BORN REM MIME TZAR** who knew **MR. OMEN** (**ZEBRA TRIM**)
MR. Z RAN ME-ORBIT-ME.	said, "**RIB ME, MR. OMEN TZAR**," do "**RIB ME, MR. ARM-TO-ZEN**!"
(I MET MR. ZEN; ARM, BRO!)	A **BORN MAZE TRIMMER**, BAND BOY L (Hey! **MR. ZEN – ARM BITER; OM**!)
MR. M RAN METEOR BIZ.	sly mordant nabob, **BY A BLOND** when ZERO **MR. MERMAN** BIT
MR. MOM RAN TREE BIZ.	Lapidifying shibboleths (Said **MR. MOM**, "**A TIN ZEE; BRR**!")
MR. IT RAN MOB, MR. ZEE.	a legendary beachcomber came **MR. IT** (**OM**!), **BRAZEN REM**
MR. ME RAN METRO BIZ.	deliveryman improbable [**MR.**] **IT NAB ZERO**, **MR. ME**
	ANY BOLD B, BLAND BOY (*What?*) (BRO, **MR. IT A ZEN MR. ME**!)
MR. M-B RAN ITEM ZERO.	immortalized submariner **MR. MIME BENT** RAZOR kept
MR. E RAN MOTE BIZ, MR.	BRR! **ATOMIZE MEN**, **MR.** E! Do BLAB, YON D; B NOBLY BAD!

INAPPROPRIATE ANAGRAMS

ANY MAIL?

MAYA LIN (b. 1959)   Artist

Arts and letters in a public place

AY, NAIL M.	Maya Lin, pure artistry	earthworks sublime, "**M**," **À LÀ YIN**
LIMY, AN A!	By minimal approach enchants	(**MY**, "**A**" **IN L.A.**! AY, **LIMN** "**A**"!)
A MANLY I.	Made *Vietnam Memorial* wall	dead *Veterans* named by **INLAY, MA**
LAMINA Y.	The casualty of war made plain	*Was not a dream,* **YIN LAMA** *showed*
AIM ANY L.	*Wave Field*, transcendent masterwork	sky touches landscape, **MY LANAI**!
"	loam hills and valleys undulate	**I, LAYMAN**, at a loss... for words
"	*Eleven Minute Line* conveys	at Wanas, twisting **MAYAN LI**
AY, MAIL N.	asemic, oundy lexigram	(Say, **ANY MAIL**? What, **MAIL**? **NAY**.)
"	*Confluence* in America	with "Story Circles" **NAILY, MA**
"	Mix native grasses, wavy frills	with history (**NAIL MAY** NAIL YAM)
LAY IN M/A.	May earth elude man's ravaging?	**AIL, MYNA**! (MANY AIL!) *Who knows?*
...	Next: Silt planet memory bank	no one will see. Grade? **MAINLY, A**

INAPPROPRIATE ANAGRAMS

Acknowledgments (**COLD MAGNETS KNEW**)

The inspiration for *Inappropriate Anagrams* and the shenanagram poetic form was an entirely unsatisfactory poem about an imaginary person that I wrote in 2009, whose iambic tetrameter (da-DUM, da-DUM, da-DUM, da-DUM), which stuck with me like an earworm, was its saving grace. Revisiting this poem as a potential candidate to share with my colleagues at the Guilford Poets Guild, I discovered that its limerick-like formula could be applied to anyone, so I dubbed the form *permutable* (you'll find this word embedded in an appropriate shenanagram, so look sharp). Writing a permutable for one of my idols, the artist Agnes Martin, I serendipitously decided to explore anagrams (I don't know why). While some of the anagrams I found were conventionally pertinent, the ones that had real magic were *in*appropriate – and delightfully provocative. This was a breakthrough. Martin yielded *Saint Engram*, *Magnet Rains* and *Mantas Reign*, and I was on my way! Scientist Madame Curie (*A Mermaid Cue* and *Um, Mare-a-Dice?*) and Queen Cleopatra (*Orca Leapt* and *Cat Parole*) quickly followed.

As an artist, I was keen to create "anagram portraits" to illustrate the surreal alter egos that the anagrams invoked. Inspired by Max Ernst's *La femme 100 têtes* and Richard Hamilton's "*Just what is it that makes today's homes so different, so appealing?*," I realized that collage, in which the juxtaposition of visual elements is transformative, was a natural fit. This visual approach, of which I was reminded by Gabriella Radujko (*Rub Jade, Koala Girl!*), is analogous to anagrams' verbal one: the shuffling of letters to transformative effect. For each collage portrait, I placed the subject's face in an associated anagrammatic scenario.

(By the way, if you have any doubts: Writing and illustrating shenanagrams is *really fun*.)

Readers, especially those who might wish to create their own shenanagrams, may find the process I utilize in creating them to be of interest. It's this: I use the *Internet Anagram Server* ("I, Rearrangement Servant"; wordsmith.org/anagram), created by alphabetician/wordplayer extraordinaire Anu Garg (*Gnu Raga*), and BestWordList.com, created by technolexicographer and wordkeeper/altruist Gilles Blanchette (*Nth Liege Bells Cat*). BIG THANKS to both. I also wish to thank Richard Prince (*Rich Id Prancer*) for finally settling the absurd question of whether *collagistes* are to be permitted to create, exhibit and sell collage, art's playful and definitively transformative genre. Citations (pp. 86-88) are provided for information only; all images are incorporated in fair use.

As to the word "Shenanagram": I wish to thank neologist *non pareil* Letitia Ferguson (*Angel Fortuities*) for coining it to capture this genre's spirit and form. I also wish to thank the several "irregulars" – poets and friends – who suggested biographical subjects for this and future volumes.

Finally, I wish to thank you, Dear Reader, for reading this book, and – if you purchased it – for supporting my creative endeavors. For the luminaries profiled herein, past and present: I wrote this book for you, too, and hope to have honored your lives with respect and good humor. As Bob Marley (*A-Bomb Lyre*) so eloquently wrote and sang, **OLÉ, OVEN**!

Constrained Poetry (ENTROPY AS DOCTRINE)

Constrained poetry, whose text follows imposed rules beyond the formal conventions of rhyme and meter – has an illustrious history. Combining the first letter in each line of Lewis Carroll's acrostic epilog poem in *Through the Looking-Glass, and What Alice Found There* produces ALICE LIDDELL, the eponymous heroine's full name (see Mary Cassatt, pp. 30-31). Notable examples of constrained poetry in the 20th Century were created by the avant-garde French *Oulipo* experimentalists Raymond Queneau (pp. 60-61), Georges Perec and others. Oulipo works included lipogrammatic texts in which specific letters were either exclusively used or entirely omitted, as in Perec's novel *La Disparition* (*A Void*), in which the letter "e" is missing. Canadian poet Christian Bök's *Eunoia* is a recent lipogrammatic prose poem *tour de force* in which a single vowel is exclusively used (univocally) in each chapter.

Nonsense poetry and prose are equally storied. Carroll's word salad "Jabberwocky" is a paradigmatic example of the former, as is Edward Lear's "The Owl and The Pussy-Cat." Their narrative nonsense and, for example, e. e. cummings's "nouns to nouns..." stand in contrast to such experimental works as Filippo Tommaso Marinetti's *parole in libertà*, Kurt Schwitters's asemic "Ursonate" sound poem and concrete poet Brion Gysin's permutational "I am," and more. Gertrude Stein's prose poem *Tender Buttons*, homaged in her shenanagram (pp. 38-39), contorts language and confounds meaning in a manner echoed in shenanagrams' constrained anagrammatic phrases.

The shenanagram, whose poetic form premieres in *Inappropriate Anagrams*, represents a new, hybrid genre – constrained text with nonsense ("inappropriate") anagrams. As a literary form, the shenanagram is distinguished by its own rules:

1. A shenanagram must be biographical and, despite appearances, accurate biographical details are mandatory.
2. Its title must end with "in a public place."
3. The first half of the first line must contain the subject's name.
4. At least eight anagrams must be used in at least four split, free verse couplets (most in iambic tetrameter), one preferably at the end of each line.
5. The words in each line, not including the line's anagram, must include every single letter in the subject's name.
6. "Appropriate" anagrams are permissible, as is rhyming.

While the creation of a complementary collage portrait to accompany a shenanagram is optional, readers will note both Surrealist and Pop Art collage (referenced in *Acknowledgments*), and the Surrealists' *cadavre exquis* ("exquisite corpse") as antecedents to, and inspirations for the collage portraits in *Inappropriate Anagrams*.

– DLC

Citations (SO TITANIC)

Frontispiece **WILD CAVE REDUNDANCY** – David Lawrence Cundy
Author: Richard Frank (2016). Tunnel of Love: Manning Amusement Park, John Kerr (undated), *East Anglian Daily Times*.

p. 2 **HULA MOAN EPÉE** – Pele Honua Mea / Madame Pele (Timeless)
Lava Lake: "High Lava Lake in Halema'uma'u," S. Geiger (April 24, 2015 between 5:00-5:30 a.m.), National Park Service. Fencer: Renée Garilhe (uncredited/1956), usfencingresults.org. "Hula hoop" (Saturn's rings): NASA and The Hubble Heritage Team (STScI/AURA), R.G. French (Wellesley College), J. Cuzzi (NASA/Ames), L. Dones (SwRI), and J. Lissauer (NASA/Ames) (1996), NASA. Aloha shirt pattern: *Willow Bough*, Wlilliam Morris (designed 1887), Metropolitan Museum of Art.

p. 4 **CAT PAROLE** – Cleopatra (69-30 BC)
Cat sarcophagus: Madam Rafaèle (2007), *Wikipedia*. Eye of Horus pendant: Jon Bodsworth (undated), *Wikipedia*. Handcuffs: George Hodan (undated), PublicDomainPictures.net.

p. 6 **CHI HEIRS KISS PINS** – Princess Shikishi (1149-1201)
Lips : *An Erotic Picture Book of Snow on Mt. Fuji*, Keisai Eisen (1824).

p. 8 **THOU A ZANY CELLO** – Nezahualcoyotl (1402-1472)
Nezahualcoyotl: Mexican 100 peso note. Cellist: Paulo Gruppe, Aimé Dupont (c. 1890-1934), Digital Commonwealth, Massachusetts.

p. 10 **SO ANIMAL** – Mona Lisa (Lisa Gherardini) (1452-1519)
Gherardini: Leonardo da Vinci (1503-1506-1517), The Louvre. Sphinx: *"Giseh. Sphinx et les pyramides des Chefren et Mankaura,"* (1870-1875), New York Public Library Digital Collections.

p. 12 **HEN HAS ABS, SIR UMP!** – (Missus) Aphra Behn (1640-1689)
Behn: Sir Peter Lely (1670), Yale Center for British Art. White Leghorn hen cigarette card: (uncredited/undated), New York Public Library Digital Collections.

p. 14 **GO! GAG THE ELF – NOW!** – Wolfgang Goethe (1749-1832)
Goethe: Angelica Kauffmann (1787), Goethe-Nationalmuseum. "Gladstone as Faust making a pact with the devil," Morgan (1885), Wellcome Collection.

p. 16 **MY EERY HALLS** – Mary Shelley (1797-1851)
Shelley: Reginal Easton (1851-1893), the Bodleian Library, University of Oxford. Castle: Stirling Castle, Scotland (uncredited/undated), HM Office of Works.

p. 18 **AHOY! A THUNDER DIVER** – Henry David Thoreau (1817-1862)
Thoreau: Benjamin D. Maxham (1856), National Portrait Gallery, Smithsonian Institution. Lightning: Steven Vanderburg (undated), National Oceanic and Atmospheric Administration. White Point Japanese abalone diver, San Pedro, California: (1905), Palos Verdes Library District.

p. 20 **NARWHALS CRIED** – Charles Darwin (1809-1882)
Darwin: T.H. Maguire (1849), the Wellcome Collection. Narwhals: *The Naturalist's Pocket Magazine* (uncredited/1800).

p. 22 **LILTING BUST** – Sitting Bull (1831-1890)
Sitting Bull: O.S. Goff (1881), State Historical Society of North Dakota. Mount Rushmore: Stephen Keegan (undated), National Archives.

p. 24 **DREAMT HAT** – Mad Hatter (b. 1865) (Lewis Carroll, 1832-1898)
Hatter: John Tenniel (1865), *Alice's Adventures in Wonderland*, Lewis Carroll (1865).

p. 26 **OH! SATAN'S BUNNY** – Susan B. Anthony (1820-1906)
Anthony: Mrs. L. Condon (between 1890-1906), Library of Congress. Bunny ears: *The Story of a Fierce Bad Rabbit,* Beatrix Potter (1906). Wallpaper fire: "Their manner of prainge vvith Ratels abowt te fyer," De Bry (1590), John Carter Brown Library at Brown University. Pitchfork: "American Gothic," Grant Wood (1930), Art Institute of Chicago. Frame: "Portrait of a Young Woman Playing a Lyre," Élisabeth-Louise Vigée-Lebrun (late 1780s), Cincinnati Art Museum.

p. 28 **MS. EEL, UNCLE SAM**! – Samuel Clemens / Mark Twain (1835-1910)
Clemens: A.F. Bradley (1907), *Wikipedia*. Moray Eel: Michael Ströck (2006), *Wikipedia*. Poster: "Boys and Girls! You can help your Uncle Sam" (uncredited/1918), Library of Virginia.

p. 30 **STAY, CAST ARM**! – Mary Cassatt (1844-1926)
Cassatt: Edgar Degas (1880-1884), National Portrait Gallery, Smithsonian Institution. Sculpture: "Venus of Capua" (uncredited/100-150 CE), Marie-Lan Nguyen (2011), Naples National Archaeological Museum, *Wikipedia*.

p. 32 **ME RADIUM ACE** – Madame Curie (1867-1934)
Curie: (uncredited/undated), George Grantham Bain Collection, Library of Congress. Pilot Marguerite Guthrie: (uncredited/undated), Hennepin County Library, Minnesota.

p. 34 **GURU'S MIND FED** – Sigmund Freud (1856-1939)
Freud: Max Halberstadt (1921). Taima Mandala: (early 14th Century), Minneapolis Institute of Art.

p. 36 **BAT RIOT EXPERT** – Beatrix Potter (1866-1943)
Potter: Rupert Potter (1881), National Trust (UK). Bats: *Art Forms of Nature,* Ernst Haeckel (1904).

p. 38 **TIGER DENTURES** – Gertrude Stein (1874-1946)
Stein: Man Ray (1922). Tiger: Cigarette card (uncredited/undated), George Arents Collection, the New York Public Library Digital Collections.

p. 40 **HAD ARK FOIL** – Frida Kahlo (1907-1954)
Kahlo: Nickolas Muray (1946), National Museum of American History, Smithsonian Institution. Halloween scene (1961): Wesselmann, Los Angeles Public Library, University of Southern California Digital Library.

p. 42 **ELITE BANNISTER** – Albert Einstein (1879-1955)
Einstein: Ferdinand Schmutzer (1922), National Library of Austria. Bannister: Carlos Heiligmann (2017), Special Collections and University Archives, University of Massachusetts Amherst Libraries.

p. 44 **DOLL NAÏF RAN RINKS** – Rosalind Franklin (1920-1958)
Franklin: (uncredited/1956), Special Collections & Archives Research Center, The Valley Library, Oregon State University. Skater: "The Skater (Portrait of William Grant)," Gilbert Stuart (1782), Andrew W. Mellon Collection, National Gallery of Art.

p. 46 **YIELD! I LOB HAIL** – Billie Holiday (1915-1959)
Holiday: William Gottleib (1946), William P. Gottlieb/Ira and Leonore S. Gershwin Fund Collection, Music Division, Library of Congress. Hail: Todd Heitkamp (2007), National Weather Service. Baseball player: The Strobridge Lith Co. (1897), Library of Congress.

p. 48 **NURSE PAM** – Superman / George Reeves (1914-1959)
Reeves: *Stamp Day for Superman* (film) (1954), Thomas Carr, director, United States Department of the Treasury. Nurse: "Nurse with a display of Abzug's Autoclavable Hospital Utensils" (undated/uncredited), Zwerdling Nursing Archives.

p. 50 **MORE MARLIN YON!** – Marilyn Monroe (1945-1962)
Monroe: Cecil Stoughton (1962), John F. Kennedy Presidential Library and Museum. Ernest Hemingway: "Ernest Hemingway posing with a marlin, Havana Harbor, Cuba" (uncredited/1934), Ernest Hemingway Collection, John F. Kennedy Presidential Library and Museum.

p. 52 **HER CAROLS CAN**! – Rachel Carson (1907-1964)
Carson: (uncredited/undated), U.S. Fish and Wildlife Service. Caroler: *Doctor Birch and His Young Friends* (1849), M.A. Titmarsh, Project Gutenberg. *Silent Spring* dust jacket: Houghton Mifflin Boston, Riverside Press (1962). Aura: Earth, GOES-16 satellite (2017), NOAA. Gold foil: "Chinese Lion," Kano Sanraku (c. 1585-1635), Honpo-Ji Temple, Kyoto.

p. 54 **DAILY NEWTS:** TILDE YAWNS – Walt Disney (1901-1966)
Disney: (1954), National Advisory Committee for Aeronautics.

p. 56 **I INK MR. ANGEL'S TRUTH** – (Rev. Dr.) Martin Luther King (Jr.) (1929-1968)
King: Dick DeMarsico (1964), New York World-Telegram and the Sun Newspaper Photograph
Collection, Library of Congress. Angel: "Border Fragment with Musical Angel" (1140-1144),
Cloisters Collection, Metropolitan Museum of Art.

p. 58 **MUD-CLEAR CHAMP** – Marcel Duchamp (1887-1968)
Duchamp: Heinrich Hoffmann (1912). Mudman: "Asaro Mudmen" (uncredited/1977),
Buffalo Museum of Science.

p. 60 **MARQUEE DAY NOUN** – Raymond Queneau (1903-1976)
Queneau: Photomaton self-portrait (c. 1929). Marquis: "Amédée-David, Comte de Pastoret,"
Jean-Auguste-Dominique Ingres (1823-1826), Art Institute of Chicago.

p. 62 **MERRY IN HELL** – Henry Miller (1891-1980)
Miller: Larry Colwell (c. 1957), National Portrait Gallery. Hell: "The Garden of Earthly Delights,"
Hieronymous Bosch (1490-1510), the Prado.

p. 64 **A-BOMB LYRE** – Bob Marley (1945-1981)
Marley: (uncredited/undated), Library of Congress. Amphora: Barbiton player, Niobid Painter
(460-450 BC), Walters Art Museum, Baltimore.

p. 66 **SIR OBOES JUGGLER** – Jorge Luis Borges (1899-1986)
Borges: (uncredited/1962), New York World-Telegram and the Sun Newspaper Photograph
Collection, Library of Congress. Juggler: "J.T. Doyle [holding 2 burning juggling clubs],"
J.E. Pasonault (c. 1902), Library of Congress. Oboes: *Famous composers and their works* (1891),
John Knowles Paine and Theodore Thomas, Editors, New York Public Library Digital Collections.

p. 68 **AH, LORD YAWN**! – Andy Warhol (1928-1987)
Warhol: Mike Mullen (1985), Herald-Examiner Collection, Los Angeles Public Library. Souvenir
card: (uncredited/c. 1950's), Richard J. Daley Collection, University of Illinois at Chicago Library.

p. 70 **HE'S RODEO LEGIT** – Theodor Geisel / Dr. Seuss (1904-1991)
Geisel: Al Ravenna (1957), Library of Congress. "The Cow Boy," John C.H. Grabill (1888),
Library of Congress.

p. 72 **SIR GEM RESORT** – Mister Fred Rogers (1928-2003)
Rogers: United States Postal Service Forever stamp (2018), Walt Seng (c. 1985). Andradite
(green): Harold and Erica Van Pelt; Beryl (yellow) and Topaz (orange): Chip Clark; Zoisite
(var. tanzanite): Greg Polley; Hope Diamond (uncredited/undated); Smithsonian Institution.
Bodies of Mister Rogers and Miss Hope Diamond: "Mr. and Mrs. William [Vanderbilt]"
(uncredited/undated), vanderbiltcupraces.com. Resort: The Alcazar, St. Augustine, Florida
(uncredited/1902), Library of Congress.

p. 74 **MAGNET RAINS** – Agnes Martin (1917-2004)
Martin: Mildred Tolbert (c. 1953). Magnets: "Sketch of 'Telegraph' Joseph Henry Showed
his Classes at the Albany Academy" (uncredited/1857), Smithsonian Institution.

p. 76 **MAD HULA IMAM** – Muhammad Ali (1942-2016)
Ali: (1969). Whirling dervish: J. Pascal Sébah (1870).

p. 78 **BORN MAZE TRIMMER** – Robert Zimmerman / Bob Dylan (b. 1941)
Dylan: At the Castle Solarium in Los Angeles, Lisa Law (1966). Hedge trimmer: "England, men on
tractor trimming road-side hedges in western Somerset," Clarence Woodrow Sorensen or Eugene
V. Harris (between 1934 and 1969), Edna Schaus Sorensen and Clarence W. Sorensen Collection,
American Geographical Society Library, University of Wisconsin-Milwaukee Libraries.

p. 80 **ANY MAIL**? – Maya Lin (b. 1959)
Lin: Walter Smith (undated). Chain mail: "Embroidered Picture," Julia Fybel (c. 1969),
Cooper-Hewitt Museum, Smithsonian Institution.